# A short account of the new pantomime called Omai, or, a trip round the world; performed at the theatre-royal in Covent-Garden. The pantomime, and the whole of the scenery, designed and invented by Mr. Loutherbourg. A new edition.

John O'Keeffe

*A short account of the new pantomime called Omai, or, a trip round the world; performed at the theatre-royal in Covent-Garden. ... The pantomime, and the whole of the scenery, designed and invented by Mr. Loutherbourg. The words written by Mr. O'keeffe; a A new edition.*
O'Keeffe, John
ESTCID: T048094
Reproduction from British Library

London : printed for T. Cadell, 1785.
[2],22p. ; 8°

Eighteenth Century
Collections Online
Print Editions

## Gale ECCO Print Editions

Relive history with *Eighteenth Century Collections Online*, now available in print for the independent historian and collector. This series includes the most significant English-language and foreign-language works printed in Great Britain during the eighteenth century, and is organized in seven different subject areas including literature and language; medicine, science, and technology; and religion and philosophy. The collection also includes thousands of important works from the Americas.

The eighteenth century has been called "The Age of Enlightenment." It was a period of rapid advance in print culture and publishing, in world exploration, and in the rapid growth of science and technology – all of which had a profound impact on the political and cultural landscape. At the end of the century the American Revolution, French Revolution and Industrial Revolution, perhaps three of the most significant events in modern history, set in motion developments that eventually dominated world political, economic, and social life.

In a groundbreaking effort, Gale initiated a revolution of its own: digitization of epic proportions to preserve these invaluable works in the largest online archive of its kind. Contributions from major world libraries constitute over 175,000 original printed works. Scanned images of the actual pages, rather than transcriptions, recreate the works *as they first appeared.*

Now for the first time, these high-quality digital scans of original works are available via print-on-demand, making them readily accessible to libraries, students, independent scholars, and readers of all ages.

For our initial release we have created seven robust collections to form one the world's most comprehensive catalogs of 18$^{th}$ century works.

*Initial Gale ECCO Print Editions collections include:*

### History and Geography
Rich in titles on English life and social history, this collection spans the world as it was known to eighteenth-century historians and explorers. Titles include a wealth of travel accounts and diaries, histories of nations from throughout the world, and maps and charts of a world that was still being discovered. Students of the War of American Independence will find fascinating accounts from the British side of conflict.

*Social Science*

Delve into what it was like to live during the eighteenth century by reading the first-hand accounts of everyday people, including city dwellers and farmers, businessmen and bankers, artisans and merchants, artists and their patrons, politicians and their constituents. Original texts make the American, French, and Industrial revolutions vividly contemporary.

*Medicine, Science and Technology*

Medical theory and practice of the 1700s developed rapidly, as is evidenced by the extensive collection, which includes descriptions of diseases, their conditions, and treatments. Books on science and technology, agriculture, military technology, natural philosophy, even cookbooks, are all contained here.

*Literature and Language*

Western literary study flows out of eighteenth-century works by Alexander Pope, Daniel Defoe, Henry Fielding, Frances Burney, Denis Diderot, Johann Gottfried Herder, Johann Wolfgang von Goethe, and others. Experience the birth of the modern novel, or compare the development of language using dictionaries and grammar discourses.

*Religion and Philosophy*

The Age of Enlightenment profoundly enriched religious and philosophical understanding and continues to influence present-day thinking. Works collected here include masterpieces by David Hume, Immanuel Kant, and Jean-Jacques Rousseau, as well as religious sermons and moral debates on the issues of the day, such as the slave trade. The Age of Reason saw conflict between Protestantism and Catholicism transformed into one between faith and logic -- a debate that continues in the twenty-first century.

*Law and Reference*

This collection reveals the history of English common law and Empire law in a vastly changing world of British expansion. Dominating the legal field is the *Commentaries of the Law of England* by Sir William Blackstone, which first appeared in 1765. Reference works such as almanacs and catalogues continue to educate us by revealing the day-to-day workings of society.

*Fine Arts*

The eighteenth-century fascination with Greek and Roman antiquity followed the systematic excavation of the ruins at Pompeii and Herculaneum in southern Italy; and after 1750 a neoclassical style dominated all artistic fields. The titles here trace developments in mostly English-language works on painting, sculpture, architecture, music, theater, and other disciplines. Instructional works on musical instruments, catalogs of art objects, comic operas, and more are also included.

**The BiblioLife Network**

This project was made possible in part by the BiblioLife Network (BLN), a project aimed at addressing some of the huge challenges facing book preservationists around the world. The BLN includes libraries, library networks, archives, subject matter experts, online communities and library service providers. We believe every book ever published should be available as a high-quality print reproduction; printed on-demand anywhere in the world. This insures the ongoing accessibility of the content and helps generate sustainable revenue for the libraries and organizations that work to preserve these important materials.

The following book is in the "public domain" and represents an authentic reproduction of the text as printed by the original publisher. While we have attempted to accurately maintain the integrity of the original work, there are sometimes problems with the original work or the micro-film from which the books were digitized. This can result in minor errors in reproduction. Possible imperfections include missing and blurred pages, poor pictures, markings and other reproduction issues beyond our control. Because this work is culturally important, we have made it available as part of our commitment to protecting, preserving, and promoting the world's literature.

**GUIDE TO FOLD-OUTS MAPS and OVERSIZED IMAGES**

The book you are reading was digitized from microfilm captured over the past thirty to forty years. Years after the creation of the original microfilm, the book was converted to digital files and made available in an online database.

In an online database, page images do not need to conform to the size restrictions found in a printed book. When converting these images back into a printed bound book, the page sizes are standardized in ways that maintain the detail of the original. For large images, such as fold-out maps, the original page image is split into two or more pages

Guidelines used to determine how to split the page image follows:

• Some images are split vertically; large images require vertical and horizontal splits.
• For horizontal splits, the content is split left to right.
• For vertical splits, the content is split from top to bottom.
• For both vertical and horizontal splits, the image is processed from top left to bottom right.

# A SHORT ACCOUNT

### OF THE

# NEW PANTOMIME

#### CALLED

# O M A I,

### O R,

## *A Trip round the World;*

##### PERFORMED AT THE

# THEATRE-ROYAL

#### I N

# COVENT-GARDEN.

##### WITH THE

## RECITATIVES, AIRS, DUETTS, TRIOS
## AND CHORUSSES,

*Written by Mr. O'Keefe*

### AND A DESCRIPTION OF THE

# PROCESSION.

The Pantomime, and the Whole of the Scenery, defigned and invented by MR. LOUTHERBOURG

The Words written by MR. O'KEEFFE;

And the Mufick compofed by Mr. SHIELDS.

### A NEW EDITION.

*LONDON*

Printed for T. CADELL, in the Strand

M DCC LXXXV.

# CHARACTERS.

Towha, the Guardian Genius of Omai's Anceftors, and Pro-
tector of the legal Kings of Otaheite, } Mrs. RIVERS.

Otoo, Father of Omai, a Defcend-
ant from the legal Kings, a Prieft and a Magician, } Mr. DARLEY.

Omai, —— Mr. BLURTON.

Otaheitean,* fuppofed to have accompanied Omai to England, } Mr. EDWIN.

Harlequin, Servant to Omai, Mr. KENNEDY.

Oediddee, Pretender to the Throne, Mrs. KENNEDY.

Oberea, Regent and Protectrefs of Oediddee, an Enchantrefs, } Mrs. MARTYR.

Britannia, —— —— Mrs. INCHBALD.

Don Struttolando, Rival to Omai, in his love to Londina, } Mr. PALMER

Clown, his Servant and Rival of Harlequin, } Mr. D'ELPINI.

Father of Londina, —— Mr. THOMPSON.

Mother, —————— Mrs DAVENETT.

Londina, the Confort deftined to Omai, —— } Mifs CRANFIELD.

Colombine, Maid to Londina, Mifs ROWSON.

Old Fairy, Friend to Harlequin, Mr. WEWITZER.

Englifh Captain, —— Mr. BRETT.

Juftice, —————— M DAVIES.

Conftables, —— Meff. { DOYLE, MEADOWS, SWORDS.

Good and Evil Spirits, Cuftom-Houfe Officers, Sailors, &c.

* The idea of his drefs was taken from Cook's Voyages, where it is faid that Omai to make himfelf fine on his return among his own dreffed himfelf from a piece of . . . of each . . . . . . from his feveral . . . . . .

# O M A I.

## P A R T  I.

SCENE I. *A Morai* (1) *in* Otaheite *by Moon-light.*

Otoo *difcovered making Invocations to the Genii of his Anceftors for their Affiftance to fix his Son on the Throne.*

RECITATIVE.——*Otoo.*

HAIL to this awful place! facred Fiatoo-
　　ka (2) hail!
Where Otaheitean Chiefs in everlafting moe (3)
　　lie; warriors renown'd,
On Eimeo's (4) fanguine plains with hard-fought
　　victory crown'd;
Tho' here in death ye moulder, yet the royal
　　line can never fail,
　　Preferv'd by Towha's power divine;
　　　　And the illuftrious name,
　　　　By glorious actions dear to fame,
In my belov'd Omai fhall never die.

(1) A temple, or burying place.
(2) A repofitory for the dead.
(3) Sleep
(4) One of the Society Iflands, generally at war with
Otaheite.

B　　　　　　　　AIR.

## A I R I.——*Otoo.*

God of Bolabola (5) hear!
Accept this plantain, yam, and hog, well roasted,
Offerings to thy Godship dear,
With mahee (6) sweet as ever boasted;
And while thus I lowly bend,
Let my humble suit ascend.

> [*The sacrifice blazes up.*

The flames arise,
Blest sacrifice!
Towha snuffs the savour;
Propitious sign
Of grace benign,
Sure token of his favor.


## R E C I T A T I V E.

Say, shall my son Omai reign?
Great Towha now an answer deign.


Towha *assumes the Appearance of a Chief
Mourner.*


## R E C I T A T I V E.—*Otoo (appalled).*

My quiv'ring flesh, my limbs bedew'd all o'er;
Each feeble sense---my eyes---my voice---no
more! [*Falls prostrate.*

---

(5) Another of the Society Islands, the most ferocious
in war, conquerors of Ulitea, which was anciently subject
to Omai's ancestors.
(6) Bread.

A I R

## AIR II.——*Towha.*

Spirits of peace that hover round,
Oh, chear his mortal sight!
Dispel with sweet responsive sound
The horrors of the night.

*[Celestial music.*

My aerial band, ar't ready?

*Chorus of spirits.* Ready.

*Tow.* To run, to swim, to fly, at my command?

*Cho.*
*Tow.* To run? Command.
*Cho.*
*Tow.* To swim? To run.
*Cho.*
*Tow.* To fly? To swim.
*Cho.*
*Tow.* At my command? To fly.
*Cho.*
Command.

Spirits *appear.*

*Tow.* His darling son with motion soft as Ma-
oaian (7) gales, hither convey
My gentle spirits away.

*Cho.*
Away!
*[Disappea*

(7) Western breezes.

*Soft Music, and* Omai *brought in.*

A I R   III —*Spirits, Otoo, and Towha.*

*Cho. (Spirits.)* Happy father---Otaheite's heir!
      [*To* Otoo *and* Omai.
*Otoo.*      Otoo's hope,
*Tow.*      And Towha's care.

R E C I T A T I V E.——*Towha.*

My precepts still from folly shall direct him,
This potent talisman from harm protect him.
   (*Places the talisman by the side of* Omai
    —*Thunder*—Britannia *is seen holding*
   Londina.)

    Britannia *speaks.*

Mark, votive Islander, thy fate is mine,
For mine
The Queen of Isles, the mistress of the main!
Upon my sea-girt shore, by Neptune fenc'd,
Kind greeting, pleasure, welcome sweet receive:
Still shall my sons, by *Cook's* example taught,
Thy new-found world protect and humanize.
In soft alliance bound, this British maid
Be thine, and Love, a radiant throne shall fix
Firm as my rock, where sits bright *Liberty.*

R E C I T A T I V E.—*Otoo.*

The splendid vision, oh, my son obey,
Towha commands  for England quick away.
        But

But ere, lov'd youth, you quit your native fhore,
Your rival Oediddee fhall reftore
The Royal Enfigns, Britain to convince
That in Omai fhe receives a Prince.

---

SCENE II. *Infide of a Morai of the antient
Aree-de-hy's* (8) *Anceftors of* Omai.

*Enter* Otoo *and* Omai.

### RECITATIVE.—*Otoo.*

[Omai *kneels.*
Alas! to fpare him you in vain implore me;
Quick, fly and bring Oediddee here before me.
[*Calls to Spirits, who bring on* Oediddee.

### RECITATIVE—*Oediddee.*

Oh, fage Otoo! accept my true contrition,
I yield obedience to each hard condition;
Your fon ftill loves me, ftill I love that fon,
From childhood ftill the race of life we've run;
My fmalleft grief was anguifh to his heart,
His flighteft joy could every joy impart.

### AIR IV——*Oediddee.*

O'er groves of coral, through the deep,
Where Mogee (9) fifh their revels keep,

(8) Grand Chiefs.
(9) An excellent fpecies of fifh in thofe feas.

Our

Our ftaunch canoes in confort glide,
Tho' ftein Farooa (10) fwells the tide,
Small the danger each could fee,
Friendfhip cried, you're fafe with me.


On the hill, that upward towers,
Crown'd with fhrubs and fweeteft flowers,
There we tafte eternal fpring,
While the Wattle-bird (11) fhall fing
Double joys to him and me,
Ever fuch let friendfhip be.


## RECITATIVE.

*Otoo.* Refign, fond youth, each filly vain pre-
  tenfion

*Oedt.* What good awaits my tacit condefcen-
  fion ?

*Otoo.* Your fortunes with my fon I'll link for
  ever

  So ftrong, that nought but death your
  fates can fever.

  Surrounding ifles fhall own thy fovereign
  fway,

  E'en diftant Wateoo * fhall tribute pay,

  Be you their Chief, their powerful
  Areekee (12)

  'T' Omai leave th' Otaheitean crown,
  this is Otoo's decree.

---

(10) A ftrong and dangerous wind
(11) The moft melodious in the Iflands.
* The fartheft fituated from Otaheite.
(12) King.

To

To Britain, now, Omai muſt repair,
And many dangers run to win the Britiſh
    fair.

### A I R V.——*Oediddee.*

Adieu, dear Omai, and gladly receive
That true and kind welcome that Britons
    can give.
                  [*General Chorus.*
Adieu, Prince Omai, and gladly receive
That true and kind welcome that Britons
    can give.

---

SCENE III. *A View of* Plymouth Sound,
*with Part of* Mount Edgcumb, *where* Omai,
*with* Harlequin *as his Servant, lands; as alſo
does* Don Struttolando, *with* Clown *as his
Servant: both in purſuit of the Object of their
Affections,* Londina. *Different comic Buſineſs
is here introduced, with the two following
Airs by an old* Water-creſs Woman, *or* Fairy.

### A I R VI.——*Old Fairy.*

Cold and hungry tho' I ſing
Water-creſſes o'the ſpring,
Your money, neighbours, little leſs is,
So buy my nice ſpring water-creſſes;
Buy my nice ſpring water-creſſes.
                    A I R

## AIR VII.——*Old Fairy.*

Keep it, prithee keep it, my kind, my generous
    Boy;
And featly, nimbly use it, fhou'd furly care
    annoy.
Quick pofting on a fun-beam, here potent
    Towha fent me;
His charge " take care of Harlequin" and
    pow'rful fpells he lent me.
    Be ftill Omai's valet, he
        With kind regard
        Shall well reward
    Thy care and ftrict fidelity.
Let pity touch thy bofom thro' frolick and va-
    gary,
And thou fhalt ever find me thy true, thy
    guardian fairy.
    [*The Scene ends with* Omai's *lofing his
    Talifman, and their going off to a Juf-
    tice of Peace for its recovery.*]

———

SCENE IV. *The* Juftice Room; *where*
Omai *gets back his Talifman, but lofes one
of his Royal Enfigns, which by fome Magic
Odour produces the Effects mentioned in the
following*

A I R VIII.——*Juftice, Captain, Conftables
and* Men.

*1ft Con.* Look here, pleafe your worfhip,
    this very fine thing,
    My eye! but it's fit for the knob of
    a King.
                     *Capt.*

*Capt.*  As you are to punish whatever's amiss,
Pray what's to be done with the stealer
of this ?

*Juft.*  I wish I may never with venison be
stuff't,
If ever I saw such a beautiful tuft !
And now, by my honor, I've thought
of a use
For this wing of a turkey, or tail of
a goose ;
'Twill make a choice top for the
head of my wife ;
It's mine, and so now there's an end
of the strife.
Oh, dear, what a delicate smell !

*1st Con.*  I vow it is wond'rous pleasing ;

*Juft.*  But why I yawn thus, I can't tell.

*1st Con.*  Oh, zounds, it has set me a sneezing.

*2d Con.*  It's a plume for a royal of France,

*1st Man.*  Or the cap of a Knight of the
Thistle.

*2d Con.*  Why what the deuce makes me thus
dance,

*1st Man.*  And tho' I've no mind I must whistle;

*2d Man.*  This perfume, good sir, let me try;

*Capt.*  A perfume indeed worth the having,

*2d Man*  Lack-a-daily, I find I must cry.

*Capt.*  By the Lord it has set me a laughing.

*All.*  To set me a { sneezing / yawning / dancing / whistling / laughing / crying } and all by a smell.

These feathers contain sure some magical spell.

C                    S C E N E

SCENE V. *A View of* Kensington Gar-
dens, *where* Omai *and* Harlequin *meet with*
Londina *and her Maid* Colombine, *and effect
their Escape together.*

---

SCENE VI. *Outside of the Father's House.*
Londina *and* Colombine *are seized by* Don
Struttolando *and* Clown, *but amidst various
Situations and much comic Business;* Harlequin
*effects an Entrance into the House, and escapes
with* Londina *and* Colombine.

---

SCENE VII. *A View of* Margate *from
behind the* Pier.---*The Company are entertain'd
by a Master of a Raffling Toy-Shop with the
following*

AIR—*Raffling Toy-Shop-Man.*

Dear Ladies and Gentlemen Customers, pop,
    will ye
Into my neat little, sweet little shop, will ye?
Walk about, Ma'am, or sit down and chat a bit;
Miss, here's the dice-box, what think you of
    that a bit?
I don't mean to gamble, or each other fleeze,
You shall only put in five and three pence a
    piece,
This enamell'd Gold Watch, tick, goes right to
    a minute;
Those lily white fingers Ma'am, surely must win it.
    Then, Ma'am, will you walk in and tol de
      rol diddle?     [*Mimicks throwing dice.*
    And, Sir, will you step in, and tol de rol diddle?
    And, Miss, will you pop in and tol de rol
      diddle?
    And, Master, pray hop in and tol de rol diddle?
              11. When

II.

When prudish, to help out your fies and your
　　hushes, Miss,
What if you throw for this bottle of blushes,
　　Miss—
Sal-Volatile, when your lover gets ranting,
You'll find, that to tip him a faint may be
　　wanting.
Ma'am, a twee that won't leave a grey hair in
　　your brow.
Sir, a wise book to read in, that's—if you
　　know how,　　　　　　　　[Aside.
Hall's, Benson's and Silver's, not saunter like
　　drones about,
But all come to Austin's, and here knock the
　　bones about.
　　　　　　　　Then, Ma'am &c.

III.

Ye Londoners, who would fling sorrow and cash
　　away,
Welcome to Margate, in Salt-water dash away.
Clean as a penny we'll souse, sop, and pickle ye;
Out of your gold, neat as Brighton we'll tickle
　　ye;
Says spousey to deary, to Margate we'll trip
In the dog-days, and give little Jacky a dip;
Tho' here in the Dilly, gay pleasure attend ye,
Yet back in the Hoy, poor as Job, we'll soon
　　send ye.
　　　　　　　　Then Ma'am &c.
Omai *and* Harlequin *with* Londina *and*
　　Colombine *leave* Europe, *and are pur-*
　　*sued, which closes the* First Part.

# PART II.

SCENE I. *A View of the* Balagans (13) *of* Kamtſchatka, *(on the Eaſtern Coaſt of* Aſia) *where* Omai *and his Party are received by the native* Kamtſchadales, *who afterwards fall into a laughable Miſtake with reſpect to the* Clown's *Appearance.*

## RECITATIVE.—*Clown.*

OH dear! am I in water, fire, air or land?
  Have I a head, leg, ſhoulder, foot or
    hand?
I muſt turn bird, the devil ſure bewitch'd me,
Whiſk'd me thro' clouds---into the ſea then
    pitch'd me.

## AIR.——*Clown.*

There Maſter Death he grinn'd ſo fierce and
    frowning,
Says I, get out you dog, I was not born for
    drowning.
Ha, ha, ha! the ladies with my dreſs would
    much be taken
In air and ſea, tho'---gad it ſav'd my bacon.

(13 Summer habitations.

SCENE

SCENE II. *Inside of a Jourt\*, where the Manners of the Natives are depicted in their Reception of* Omai *and his Suit, by dancing and singing the following*

GLEE.——AIR IX.——*Natives.*

Give me thy paw, my bonny bonny bear,
   And here come dip thy muzzle;
Tho' a good warm coat thy back doth wear,
  When tempests blow
  The drifted snow,
Oh that's the time for a merry merry sup,
So we'll chear our hearts with a chirping cup,
   And close together nuzzle.
When the North-wind whistles we dance to the
  note,
   We quiver
    And we quaff,
   We shiver
    And we laugh
At the chrystal beard that hangs from the goat.
 [*At the end of which,* Harlequin *having lost*
  Londina *and* Maid, *changes the whole
  Habitation to*

    \* Winter habitation.

SCENE III. *A dreary* Ice Island, *where the Parties encounter a Variety of Dangers, and escape to*

---

SCENE IV. *A* Village *in* Tongataboo, *the most beautiful and considerable of the* Friendly Islands.

*The Natives enter, fabricating their feathered Garments, and singing the following*

## RONDEAU *and* CHORUS.

Plenty gives, and pleasure smiles,
O'er our happy Friendly Isles;
While so blest, what should we do
But sing, O sweet Tongataboo?

On this green and fragrant spot,
Down we here together squat,
With our scarlet plumage crown'd,
While the kava-bowl (14) goes round.

      Plenty gives, &c.

Here in shades of wharra-palms, (15)
Cocoa-milk, delicious yams;
Dance the mai, (16) naffa, (17) beat
Nimble pagge, (18) tune our feet,

      Plenty gives &c.

(14) An intoxicating liquor.
(15) A particular palm
(16) A grand dance.
(17) A musical drum
(18) An instrument with which they beat time in their dances.

          Omai

Omai *and* Harlequin, *after Comic Bufinefs,* go *off with their Ladies ; and* Don Struttolando, Father, *and* Clown, *are guided by a Native, in purfuit to*

————————

SCENE V. *A confecrated Place in the Sandwich Iflands, where* Oberea *the En-chantrefs ftops the Purfuit by*

RECITATIVE.———*Oberea.*

Forbear, rafh mortals, nor with unhallow'd foot
    profane
The facred morai---ftop, on pain
      Of inftant death !——
     [Indian *acquaints* Oberea *of their purfuit of* Omai, *to whom fhe is an Enemy.*]

RECITATIVE *accompanied*——*Oberea.*

  Cheer thy heart, be not afraid;
  Truft, by Oberea's aid
  Londina thou fhalt foon recover
  From her wild and vagrant lover;
  For my favourite Oediddee,
  Of Omai's pranks I'll rid ye.

*They all go off in fearch to*

SCENE VI. *Another Part of the Sand-wich Iflands, where the Natives are enter-tained, by an* Otaheitean Traveller, *with the following*

3              A I R

AIR.——*Otaheitean Traveller.*

In de big canoe
I o'er ocean swim me,
Jack and merry crew
Give good liquor to me.
Over sand and rocks
Teach me sail, no paddle;
Teach me den to box,
So to use my daddle.  Tol, lol, lol, &c.
Oh! I suck'd the grog,
Brandy, gin, and rumme,
Vid de jolly dog,
Den to London comme;
Vat you tink of dat:
Rice my hair did powder,
Rub my head vid fat,
Dat's to make me prowder  Tol, lol, lol, &c.
Snug as littel mouse
From de vind and veather,
Drag'd about in house
Made of trus and leather:
To de woman fair
Up de stair I trottee;
She did sit on chair,
On the floor I squattee.  Tol, lol, lol, &c.
But dis lady fine
Call me ugly divil,
Guinea, glass of wine,
Den so tweet and civil,
In her spousy jump
As of kiss I beg her,
Give my head de tunip,
Cry, get out dam Negar.  Tol, lol, lol, &c.

*Omai is driven to great Distress, and to the
Exercise of his Magic Power, which forms*
SCENE

SCENE VII. *Where he escapes from his Enemies to* Otaheite, *and is pursued by* Oberea, *&c.*

---

SCENE VIII. *A* Moon-light Scene *in a sequester'd Part of* Otaheite.

Oberea *and the* Pursuers *enter:*

RECITATIVE, *accompanied ---Oberea.*

Soft and lightly tread, as falling snow upon the
    Hoohoo's (19) wing.
        In this delicious spot
  By sweet Kabulla's (20) op'ning odours
    richly perfum'd,
Where creeping taro (21) and ehoee (22) spring;
Where dancing shadows chequer the carpet of
    this green alcove,
Favor'd retreat of wild Omai, Londina fair,
    and love.
Here my spells are planted without number,
When sweet delusive airs shall lull each sense to
    slumber.

   (19) A beautiful bird of these islands.
   (20) A delicate and fragrant flower.
   (21) Bread-fruit
   (22) A sweet scented shrub.

### AIR.——*Oberea.*

Lightning's flash, and thunder's roll,
Swell the tumults of my soul
To wicked Etee's (23) altar bear them,
With tooth of shark in piece-meal tear them;
Burn, consume, and feast my eyes
With the blazing sacrifice.*
[*They retire, and Omai's followers fall into
the fire.*

SCENE IX. Oberea's Dwelling, (*full of
magical Instruments, &c*) Oberea *prepares to
wreak her Vengeance on Omai, but is counter-
acted by* Towha.

### Towha *speaks.*

Hold! the fatal pooa (24) drop!
Taking Omai's life, you kill your friend,
For know, their vital threads I've interwoven——
here end
Strife, hate, contending emulation,
Confirm their generous reconciliation;
And on that sordid wretch, his persecutor,
hurl thy indignation.

(23) An evil spirit
* Human sacrifice in Otaheite.
(24) Pahooa, the weapon of an Otaheitean warrior.

Oberea

RECITATIVE *accompanied, Oediddee, &c.*

Oh, potent Obèrea! now extend
Thy kind protection to my much lov'd friend.
*Otoo.* Omai's union with the British fair, god-
deſs ratify.
*Oberea.* Content!
*Otoo.*                    Then peace,
*Oedid.*                         And love,
*All.* And harmony ſhall crown the nuptial tie.
                    [*Oberea joins their hands.*
          [*Clouds aſcend, and the whole ſtage changes
              to the Laſt Scene.*

R E C I T A T I V E.

*Oedid.*  Vaſſals, to your lawful Prince of Ota-
heite
*Otoo.*  Ye tribes of Ulitea, Mataia, Mataeva,
Huaheine (25)
Hear! Ye people ſcatter'd o'er the wide
Pacific Main.

T R I O.——*Oediddee, Oberea and Otoo.*

Nations, warriors, chiefs renown'd,
From the diſtant iſles around
Aſſemble all, and hail your King,
Sound the Conch (26) let triumph ring.

(25) Iſlands.
(26) A ſhell, uſed as a trumpet.

A *Views*

*A View of the* Great Bay *of* Otaheite *at* Sun-fet.
On one fide a Magic Palace——the Bay filled
with ships and boats, bringing the Deputies
from the different quarters of the globe that
have been vifited by Capt. Cook, &c. bearing
prefents and congratulations to Omai, on his
advancement to the throne of his Anceftors, and
who afterwards approach him dreffed charac-
terifically, according to their feveral countries,
in the following

# PROCESSION.

*An* Eatooa * *addreffes* Omai.

\* A mad Prophet.

TRANSLATION ——" Ambaffadors and Plenipos,
here fwear fealty in the name of all your States to Prince
Omai, who has travelled farther than ever canoe paddled,
to the Country of mighty George, whofe great fword in
the hand of Elliott, keeps the Strong Rock from the rich
King of Lima, even in his own land. Know all, that
Omai is owner of fifty red feathers, mafter of four hundred
fat hogs; he can command a thoufand fighting men, and
twenty ftrong-handed women to thump him to fleep, and
I, your Prophet, prophecy, that thefe fupreme delights,
by George's aid, Omai ne'er fhall want' All Reverence

I.

A dancing Girl of *Otaheite*.
Six Men of *Otaheite* (as Attendants preceding)

II.

One Chief of *New Zealand*.
Two Warriors     ditto.
One common Man, ditto.
One Woman with a Child, ditto.

III.

One Chief of *Tanna*.
Two Men of ditto.
One Woman of ditto.

IV.

One Chief of *Marquesas*.
Two Men of ditto.

V.

One Chief of *Friendly Islands*.
Four Men of ditto.

VI.

One Chief of *Sandwich Islands*.
Seven Men of ditto (plain Helmets.)
One Chief of ditto (feathered Helmets.)
Seven men of ditto (with ditto.)

4                    VII. One

### VII.

One Chief of *Easter Island*.
Two Men of ditto.

### VIII.

One Chief of *Tschutzki Tartars*.
Four Men of ditto.
One Woman of ditto.

### IX.

One Russian.
Two Russian Women.

### X.

One Chief of *Kamtschatka*.
Four Men of ditto.
One Woman and a Child, ditto.

### XI.

Two Men of *Nootka Sound*.
One Woman of ditto.

### XII.

Two Men of *Oonalashka*.
One Woman of ditto.

### XIII.

Two Men of *Prince William's Sound*.
One Woman of ditto.

### XIV.

The Otaheitean Girl with Presents to the
    Captain.
Twelve Otaheitean Dancers.

### XV.

The English Captain and Sailor.

Capt.

Ingram Content Group UK Ltd.
Milton Keynes UK
UKHW030630200323
418846UK00008B/583